THE FARM ANIMALS

LES ANIMAUX DE LA FERME

BY SARAH BUFKENS

QUELS ANIMAUX TROUVE-T-ON
À LA FERME?

WHAT ANIMALS DO WE FIND
ON THE FARM?

LE CHEVAL

THE HORSE

LA VACHE

THE COW

LE TAUREAU

THE BULL

L'ÂNE

THE DONKEY

LE MOUTON

THE SHEEP

LA CHÈVRE

THE GOAT

LE COCHON

THE PIG

LE CHIEN

THE DOG

LE CHAT

THE CAT

LA POULE

THE CHICKEN

LE CANARD

THE DUCK

LE CIGNE

THE SWAN

LA DINDE

THE TURKEY

L'OIE

THE GOOSE

LE LAPIN

THE RABBIT

LA SOURIS

THE MOUSE

LE CORBEAU

THE CROW

LA CHOUETTE

THE BARN OWL

L'ABEILLE

THE BEE

PRONUNCIATION GUIDE

Page 01: La ferme (lah FER-meh)
Page 02: Le cheval (leh she-VAL)
Page 03: La vache (lah vahsh)
Page 04: Le taureau (leh TO-roh)
Page 05: L'âne (lAhn)
Page 06: Le mouton (leh moo-TON)
Page 07: La chèvre (lah shehvr)
Page 08: Le cochon (leh CO-shon)
Page 09: Le chien (leh she-EHN)
Page 10: Le chat (leh shah)
Page 11: La poule (lah pool)
Page 12: Le canard (leh can-AR)
Page 13: Le cigne (leh SE-gne)
Page 14: La dinde (lah Deyhn-de)
Page 15: L'oie (lwoah)
Page 16: Le lapin (leh lah-PEHN)
Page 17: La souris (lah su-REE)
Page 18: Le corbeau (leh COR-bo)
Page 19: La chouette (lah shoo-ET)
Page 20: L'abeille (lA-bay)

LE DÉFI DE L'AUTEUR
AUTHOR'S CHALLENGE

Activité: Peux-tu trouver Waldo l'escargot (l'ES-cargoh)?

Activity: Can you find Waldo the snail?

Dear Parents,

Reading is such a crucial part of our children's cognitive development. Not only do they develop listening skills, language skills and literacy, they tap into a limitless world of imagination and creativity. Having grown up in a bilingual household, and being a bookworm myself, I wished to create a short book that would combine culture, imagination, and language.

The goal of this book is to encourage the bilingual learning of the English and French language while fostering the love for reading. The use of simple words alongside beautiful watercolor imagery, creates the perfect introductory book to these two languages. Please refer to the pronunciation guide if you yourself are new to the French language.

I wish you many hours of viewing, reading, and story telling pleasure. Enjoy!

Sarah Bufkens

OUR ANIMAL SERIES

THE FARM ANIMALS

COMING SOON

THE FOREST ANIMALS

CREATED BY SARAH BUFKENS

EDITED BY STEPHENIE BECKER

www.ingramcontent.com/pod-product-compliance
Ingram Content Group UK Ltd.
Pitfield, Milton Keynes, MK11 3LW, UK
UKHW061459070726
13610UKWH00003B/5

* 9 7 9 8 9 9 0 0 4 8 1 1 9 *